LOOKING AFTER YOUR PET
Fish

Text by Clare Hibbert
Photography by Robert and Justine Pickett

an imprint of Hodder Children's Books

Titles in the LOOKING AFTER YOUR PET series:

• Cat • Dog • Hamster • Rabbit • Guinea Pig • Fish

© 2004 White-Thomson Publishing Ltd

Produced by White-Thomson Publishing Ltd
2/3 St Andrew's Place, Lewes, BN7 1UP

Editor: Elaine Fuoco-Lang
Inside design: Leishman Design
Cover design: Hodder Wayland
Photographs: Robert Pickett
Proofreader: Alison Cooper

Published in Great Britain in 2004 by Hodder
Wayland, an imprint of Hodder Children's Books.

Hodder Children's Books
An imprint of Hodder Headline Limited
338 Euston Road, London, NW1 3BH

British Library Cataloguing in Publication Data
Hibbert, Clare
    Fish. - (Looking after your pet)
    1. Aquarium fishes - Juvenile literature
    2. Aquariums - Juvenile literature
    I.Title
    639.3'4

ISBN 0 7502 4301 5

Acknowledgements
With thanks to Fabrice Mascart of Vanishing
World, Herne Bay, Kent and Aquatic Warehouse,
Herne Bay, Kent.

Cover image: Michael Keller/Corbis

The website addresses (URLs) included in this
book were valid at the time of going to press.
However, because of the nature of the Internet,
it is possible that some addresses may have
changed, or sites may have changed or closed
down since publication. While the author,
packager and publisher regret any inconvenience
that this may cause readers, no responsibility for
any such changes can be accepted by either the
author, the packager or the publisher.

Printed in China

Contents

Choosing fish

The first question to ask yourself is "why do I want fish?"

Fish are beautiful to watch and make brilliant pets, especially if you are allergic to fur or feathers. But before you decide to keep fish, check that you are willing to look after them. Coldwater fish, such as goldfish, are not very expensive – but their tank can be. You must also find time to feed your fish every day, and clean their tank every fortnight.

◀ A clean tank, stocked with healthy fish and plants, is a beautiful thing to watch.

A goldfish can live for eight years or more but goldfish have been known to live for over 40 years (see page 29). You will be responsible for looking after it for all that time. Whenever you go on holiday, you will need to find someone to care for your pet.

▲ If you want to keep tropical freshwater fish, you will have to heat the water in the tank.

Pet Talk

What kind of fish would you like to keep?

• Coldwater fish include goldfish and shubunkins. These are the best pets for beginners.

• Tropical freshwater fish include tetras and guppies. They need warm water, so they are trickier to care for. See pages 24–27 for information about tropical freshwater fish.

▲ Shubunkins are happy in cold water and have beautiful patterns and colouring. This one has a fancy fantail.

Tank talk

Set up your tank before you get your fish.

You need to check the new equipment and let the water and plants settle so everything is ready for your new fish.

Tanks are sold in aquariums (specialist fish shops), pet shops and garden centres – or look in your local paper for a cheaper, second-hand one. A tank 60 cm long, 30 cm wide and 40 cm deep can house five or six coldwater fish.

▼ When choosing a fish tank try and get the largest one possible.

▲ Do not be tempted by a pretty goldfish bowl. It is too small, and its narrow neck will not allow enough oxygen into the water.

The tank should have a lid (with a fitted light). This will stop your fish jumping out and keep dust off the water. You will also need an electric air pump and filter to keep the water clear.

Checklist: fish kit

- Glass (or tough plastic) tank with lid and fitted fluorescent tube light
- Air pump
- Filter
- Pea gravel
- Plants
- Fish food
- Net

- Rocks or wood (but no sharp edges)

- Feeding ring (optional)
- Two thermometers: one to fix inside the tank and one to test water refills
- Cleaning kit including siphon (see pages 18-19)

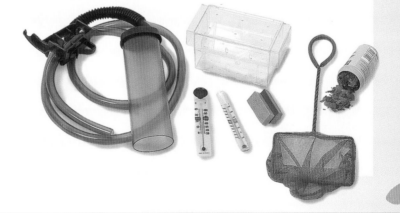

Setting up home

Put the tank in its final place before you fill it with water.

First clean the tank, to get rid of any dust. Use plain, not soapy, water. Rinse the gravel and use it to line the bottom of the tank. Add some larger stones for your fish to hide behind.

Tap water contains a gas called chlorine that can kill fish. Leave tap water in a bucket for 24 hours, so the chlorine escapes. If you prefer, buy dechlorinating tablets from the pet shop to make the water safe.

▼ Give your new tank a good clean and rinse. It is surprising how dusty it can get in the shop.

Top Tips

Where to put your tank

 Put the tank on a steady surface – when it is full of water, it will be very heavy.

Position the tank away from radiators or bright sunshine.

Keep the tank out of reach of cats and other pets.

Make sure you can reach the tank for feeding and cleaning.

◀ Make sure your tank is at a good height for you, so that you are able to feed your fish and clean out their tank. It should be on a sturdy table that can take the weight of all the water.

Plant life

Plants help to keep your tank healthy.

Plants help your fish by putting extra oxygen into the water. Oxygen is the gas animals breathe to stay alive.

Ask staff in the pet shop how many plants you will need for your size of tank. Rinse the plants first. Put them into the tank when it is half-full. Some water plants come in plastic baskets. Others have bare roots. Bury the basket or roots under the gravel.

▶ To put in your plants, first scoop a dip in the gravel for the basket. Pile gravel around it to hold it steady in the water.

Ask an adult to set up the filter and light and check any wiring. Then top up the tank with more dechlorinated water. Leave the tank for a couple of days. Check that the pump and filter are working well.

▶ You can put your plants anywhere you like. They will make an underwater forest for your pet fish.

Checklist: plant life

Here are some plants for coldwater tanks. Don't worry if you forget the names – you can always ask for advice in the shop.

- Arrowhead (Sagittaria)
- Cardinal flower (Lobelia cardinalis)
- Eel grass (Vallisneria gigantean)
- Java fern (Microsorum)
- Java moss (Vesicularia dubyana)

- Peace lily (Spathyphyllum)
- Pennywort (Hydrocotyle)
- Swordplant (Aponogeton)
- Waterweed (Elodea densa)

▲ Waterweed (Elodea densa)

▲ Cardinal flower (Lobelia cardinalis)

▲ Eel grass
(Vallisneria gigantean)

Buying your fish

There are more types of coldwater fish than you might think!

Ordinary goldfish are handsome and hardy. They come in shades of red, orange and yellow. There are also all sorts of fancy goldfish, including orandas, fantails, veiltails and comets. You could try a dark, velvety moor or a colourful shubunkin.

Other coldwater fish that make good pets include weather loach, bitterling, danios, barbs and ricefish. The aquarium staff will help you choose.

▼ Spend time looking at the fish before you choose any. Only pick ones that look healthy and strong.

It is best to put new fish in your tank in stages, one or two at a time. You should leave the new fish in for about a week so they can settle before adding any more.

▶ The aquarium staff will put your new pet in a plastic bag half-filled with water. Your fish will be fine in the bag for a short time.

Top Tips

Choosing a healthy fish

Make sure you buy your fish from a pet shop or aquarium that takes good care of its animals.

🐟 The fish should be active, not lurking near the bottom.

🐟 It should swim steadily, not tilt to one side.

🐟 Its fins should be straight, not floppy.

🐟 Its body should be well filled-out, but its belly should not be swollen.

🐟 Its scales should be smooth and flat, with no white fluff or spots.

▲ Orandas are fancy goldfish that have a bulge on the top of the head. This one is called a red cap oranda – it is easy to see why.

Settling in

Never tip new fish straight into the tank.

The shock could kill your fish. Float the bag on the surface so that its water can reach the same temperature as the tank water. After about 20 minutes, unknot the bag and roll down the sides. When the water in the bag and the tank are at the same temperature, let a little tank water trickle into the bag.

◄ When you are carrying your new pet home, hold the bag carefully. Make sure there is enough water at the bottom for your fish.

Eventually you can tip the bag. Once the fish swim out, remove the bag from the water.

Keep the tank light off for the first day. This will give the fish a chance to rest after their journey. After this, turn the light on each morning and turn it off each evening – to give your fish 'day' and 'night'.

▼ Use your thermometers to test the water temperatures in the bag and the tank.

Top Tips

Your new fish

Never touch your fish. You could damage their scales. Always use a net.

Sudden temperature changes are very bad for fish.

Ask at the shop if your fish have been quarantined (kept away from other fish) to check for disease. If not, keep them in a separate tank for two weeks.

Feeding your fish

Feed your fish at the same time each day.

You can buy goldfish food from pet shops. Never overfeed your fish. Follow the instructions on the goldfish food tub and take away any uneaten food after ten minutes. If food sinks to the bottom, it makes the water dirty. You could also use a feeding ring (see page 30), which will make clearing away any leftover food much easier.

▼ Your pets will soon learn when it's dinner-time. They will come to the surface when you feed them.

Pet Talk

Going on holiday?

You can buy special food tablets that slowly release food for your fish. These are fine, but it is better to ask a friend or neighbour to come and feed your fish. At the same time they may be able to spot and treat any signs of illness.

Goldfish can eat other food, too. Try tiny pieces of lettuce and spinach, or even a few oats. These foods help fish that are constipated.

Fish love live food. You can buy this in aquariums. The two main types are daphnia (water fleas) and tubifex worms (bloodworms).

▶ You can buy live food in bags from your local aquarium. Your pets will love chasing water creatures like these daphnia (water fleas).

Cleaning the tank

It is your job to keep your pets' home clean.

Droppings and uneaten food make the water dirty, but you cannot change all the water at once. Replace about a fifth of the tank water every fortnight. Use a plastic tube to siphon the water into a bucket.

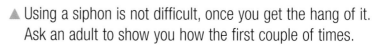
▲ Using a siphon is not difficult, once you get the hang of it. Ask an adult to show you how the first couple of times.

Move the siphon through the gravel so it can suck up all the waste settled at the bottom.

Next, net the fish and pop them in the bucket of siphoned water. Scrape off any green from the sides of the tank and remove any dead plants. Put back the fish and then, a little at a time, top up the tank with clean, dechlorinated water.

◀ You can clean the tank with the fish in it, but it is much easier to move them into a bucket of siphoned-off water.

◀ Treat the new water to get rid of chlorine. Use a dechlorinator or leave the water to stand in a bucket for 24 hours.

Top Tips

Cleaning the filter

When you clean the tank, check the filter, too. The filter helps to keep the tank clear by sucking waste from the water. Ask an adult to help you remove the foam or wool. Rinse in water from the tank or, if it is very dirty, replace it.

Sickness and health

You can help prevent disease by keeping the tank clean.

You should also check on the health of your fish at least once a day. If your fish has white fluff on its body, it probably has a fungal disease. Another problem is white spot, caused by a tiny pest living on your pet. Pet shops sell treatments for these diseases that you put in the water. If you can, move the sick fish into a separate recovery tank – the others might pick on it if it seems weak or catch the disease themselves.

Although it is difficult to take a fish to the vet, you can still ask your vet for advice. He or she may even make a home visit.

▲ This fish has white spot on its fins, head and gills. Eventually the disease will cover its entire body.

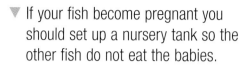
If your fish become pregnant you should set up a nursery tank so the other fish do not eat the babies.

Pet Talk

Small fry

Healthy, happy fish might have babies! Goldfish lay tiny eggs, which stick to the leaves of plants. The adults often eat the eggs or baby fish, which are called fry. If you want the eggs to hatch, move them to a nursery tank (a small tank without any adult fish).

Pond fish

Some fish are happy to live outside.

If you are lucky enough to have a pond, why not keep fish in it? You can also build your own – ask an adult to help. Make it at least 60 cm deep, so that not all the water freezes in winter. Use a tough pond liner to contain the water.

▼ Put plants in your pond. Your fish can hide among the stems – and even nibble at them, too.

Common goldfish, comets and some shubunkins can all live in outdoor ponds. So can koi carp. These are beautiful relatives of the goldfish. The large ones can be very expensive. Thieves have been known to steal koi carp, so they are not a good choice if your pond is in the front garden!

▶ With their beautiful markings, it is no wonder that koi carp are such popular pond pets. Koi can grow to 30 cm or more if they have enough space.

▼ Sometimes birds come and steal your pond fish. If you have this problem, you may need to cover your pond with a net.

Top Tips

Outdoor ponds

🐟 A pond is a bad idea if you have younger brothers or sisters. They could fall in.

🐟 Site the pond away from overhanging trees, or put a net over it to catch fallen leaves.

🐟 Stock your pond with plants for your fish to eat and use as shelter.

🐟 Cover your pond with a net if birds or cats are hunting your fish.

Totally tropical

Tropical fish come in all sorts of amazing colours and shapes.

However, they need more equipment than coldwater fish. As well as a tank, lid, light, filter and pump, you will also need a heater and thermostat. The heater warms the water. Position this near the air pump. The thermostat controls the heater to keep the water temperature steady.

▼ Set the thermostat to keep the water in your tropical tank at 24ºC. You should check this on the thermometer on the outside of the tank.

The best place to buy tropical fish is at an aquarium. Ask the aquarist to help you choose the right equipment – and the right fish for your tank. Remember to buy some plants and tropical fish food, too.

▶ Tetras like to swim together in shoals. Neon tetras like these have a light-catching stripe along their body.

Checklist: plant life

Here are a few of the plants that are suitable for tropical tanks. Your aquarist will be able to make some suggestions, too.

- Amazon sword (Echinodorus paniculatus)
- Brazilian elodea (Egeria densa)
- Dwarf anubias (Anubias barteri)
- Dwarf crypt (Cryptocoryne willisii)

- Fanwort (Cabomba aquatica)
- Marble Queen (Echinodorus cordifolius)
- Pennywort (Hydrocotyle leucocephalia)
- Tropical sun (Hygrophila rosanervis)

▲ Amazon sword

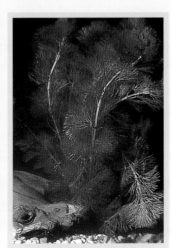

▲ Fanwort

▲ Marble Queen

▲ Tropical sun

Types of tropical fish

Choose fish that swim and feed at different depths.

▲ Angelfish have flat bodies and elegant, long pointed fins.

You need hardy fish that will live happily together. Choose fish that like to live and feed at different levels of the tank, then the fish can all live together happily and have more room to swim about.

Surface feeders are fast-moving and have upturned mouths. They include the zebra danio, the glass catfish and the Siamese fighting fish. Midwater fish stick to the middle of the tank. There are fast-moving tetras and barbs, as well as angelfish and gouramis.

▲ The golden gourami is a peaceful fish, but it is best not to keep two males in the tank together – one might bully the other.

Bottom feeders usually have a down-turned mouth and a flat underside. They suck food from the tank's bottom and sides – and help keep it clean! They include the clown loach, plecs and some catfish, such as the suckermouth.

◀ Plecs stick to the bottom of the tank, hoovering up any algae that is growing there. Choose carefully, though. Some plecs can grow to be 60 cm long – or more.

Pet Talk

Tropical types

There are two types of tropical fish – freshwater and marine. Marine fish are used to living in the sea. Because they need the right amount of salt in the water, as well as the right temperature, they are best left to the experts. When buying tropical fish, check that you are buying freshwater ones.

▼ A tank stocked with fish that feed at different levels is called a community tank.

Fish facts

Bet you didn't know that Egyptian pharaohs kept coldwater fish in their palaces! Read on for more fantastic facts.

- Chinese emperors were keeping pet fish in ponds around 1,000 years ago. They took the hobby to Japan 500 years ago.

- Europeans began keeping pet fish in the late 1600s, after explorers came back from the East with tales of the beautiful ponds they had seen.

- Tropical fish come from a warm part of the world called the tropics – the area between two imaginary lines that circle the Earth, called the Tropic of Cancer and the Tropic of Capricorn.

- There are over 100 different kinds of goldfish.

- Most pet fish are harmless, but some people keep piranhas! Piranhas come from South American rivers. A shoal of them can strip an animal to the bone in minutes.

- A pregnant goldfish is called a twit.

- The record for the longest-living goldfish is held by Goldie, which celebrated its 43rd birthday in January 2003.

- Goldfish fry are browny-grey. It can take a year for them to turn orange. In their last years, goldfish sometimes turn silvery.

- Pond fish hibernate when the weather gets really cold. Their body slows right down and they do not need to eat. They become active again in the summer, when temperatures start to rise.

Glossary

Air pump
A machine that pumps bubbles of air into the tank. The movement of water helps to create more oxygen and gives the fish a current to swim against.

Algae
A kind of seaweed that grows in aquariums.

Allergic
Having a bad reaction (such as a skin rash or difficulty breathing) to something – such as fur, feathers, dust or a certain type of food.

Aquarist
Someone who works in a shop that sells pet fish.

Aquarium
(1) A fish tank. (2) A shop that sells pets that live in tanks, such as fish and terrapins. (3) A fish zoo, where there are tanks of fish on display.

Chlorine
A type of gas that is put in tap water to kill germs. However, it can also kill fish, so only ever use dechlorinated water in your tank.

Coldwater fish
Fish that come from cooler waters, such as goldfish. Coldwater fish are used to water temperatures between 12°C and 24°C.

Constipated
Not able to go to the toilet properly.

Dechlorinator
A tablet or liquid that can be added to water to remove the chlorine and make it safe for fish tanks.

Feeding ring
A plastic ring that floats on the surface of the tank. Sprinkle a pinch of fish food inside the ring to make it easier to clear away uneaten fish food.

Filter
A machine in the tank that takes in water, sieves out particles of dirt and then puts back the cleaned water.

Fluorescent
A type of light suitable for fish tanks because it does not heat up like an ordinary light bulb.

Freshwater fish
A fish that comes from rivers or lakes, rather than the sea.

Fry
Young fish.

Heater
A machine used to heat the water in a tropical fish tank.

Hibernate
Enter a sleep-like state. Pond fish often hibernate during the cold winter months.

Marine fish
A fish that comes from the sea, rather than rivers or lakes, so it is used to being in salty water.

Oxygen
A gas that all animals need to breathe. You take in oxygen from the air using your lungs. Fish take in oxygen from the water using their gills.

Quarantined
When an animal, such as a fish, is kept away from other animals in case they are carrying a disease.

Siphon
A plastic tube that can be used to suck up water from the tank.

Thermostat
A machine used to control a heater. It can keep the temperature in a tropical tank steady.

Tropical fish
Fish that are used to warmer waters, for example tetras. Most tropical fish are happy in water temperatures around 24-27°C.

Further information

Books

Looking After My Pet Goldfish by Helen Piers
(Francis Lincoln, 2002)

Me and My Pet: Goldfish by Christine Morley and Carole Orbell
(Two-Can Publishing, 1997)

Pets: Goldfish by Michaela Miller
(Belitha, 2000)

Useful addresses

PDSA
Whitechapel Way
Priorslee
Telford
Shropshire
TF2 9PQ
Tel: 01952 290999
Fax: 01952 291035
Website: www.pdsa.org.uk

RSPCA
Wilberforce Way
Southwater
Horsham
West Sussex
RH13 9RS
Tel: 0870 3335 999
Fax: 0870 7530 284
Website: www.rspca.org.uk

Index